LIZBETH D'LEON

My Katie-Mate
The Jack Russell That Stole My Heart

Contents

One

Finding Katie

It was not an easy time in my life. My partner had left me right before I had to have back surgery. I was already afraid because you only heard horror stories about having your back operated on and I had been in pain for over a year. Sometimes it would be days at a time where I couldn't get out of bed. There was always a constant pain down my right leg so I finally went to a doctor.

The doctor confirmed that my back was not good. The disk that sits on your sacrum was gone, degenerated they said. My backbone was moving around on the sacrum instead of being in a single spot like it should be. After the x-rays, he did a simple test on me by placing the ball of my foot on his hand and asking me to resist as he pushed it forward but I couldn't resist no matter how hard I tried.

The surgery took bone from my hip and fused it to my back bone in place of my disk. It went well and that very day after recovery, the doctor came in and did the same simple test. He asked me to resist as he pushed against the ball of my foot and I could with ease. The bad dreams I had had about them cutting into my back and finding nothing wrong were no longer applicable. For the first time, I was happy I had it done even with all the anxiety I had felt up to that very moment.

My sister took me home when I got out of the hospital and I went through my recovery alone at my house. I started to become depressed from the breakup and being laid up did not help. I was feeling very suicidal and I let me sister know the day I took out every pill I had with the intention of taking them. I looked at those pill jars on my bathroom counter and knew I had to let someone know so that I wouldn't do something I would regret.

My sister would check in with me daily until I started feeling better. I started walking during the first week after surgery. Eventually I was up to five miles and once I had recovered enough to return to work, I did. But another blow was about to hit. Sometimes it seems that when you're down is when you get hit the hardest.

Work welcomed me back with open arms and I got full into it and why not, I'm a workaholic. I was starting to feel that I needed a companion and I wasn't quite ready for a human one just yet so I decided to get a puppy. I looked online for someone selling Jack Russells which is a favorite breed of mine. Soon I had a little man by my side named Frankie. He was a smooth coat, all white except for his eye and ear which were gray. Gray is not a standard color for Jacks.

I started going to JRTCA (Jack Russell Terrier Club of America) trail events where Frankie loved to try and catch a plastic bag. Yes, a plastic bag. They had a boxed maze course setup with a lure machine that had a rope with a plastic bag tied to the end of it. It cost a few dollars to let your dog run (any dog could do it) and they would chase down that plastic bag which was always just out of reach. Frankie loved it! It was at one of these events that a litter of Jack Russells were being sold.

Oh, they were beautiful tri-colored dogs and I saw one I wanted so much. She was an adorable little smooth coated, tri-colored girl but there was a wait list. I was not high on that list but I jotted down my name all the same with high hopes.

It was about two weeks later that I got a call from the breeder who advised me that the little one I wanted already got a home but she had one little pup left if I wanted her. I didn't remember this one but I told her I would take her and just hoped she would be as cute as the one I had wanted. Two days later, the breeder brought her to my house and introduced me to this small (runt of the litter) broken coated, tri-colored pup and one look at her and she had my heart. Little did I know just how much she would take a permanent place there.

I named her Kaitlyn Elizabeth, Katie for short.

Two

The Long Fall

Frankie and Katie got along really well. Katie slept through the night and was so easy to train. It was as if she already knew what she was supposed to do, but Frankie, he was stubborn and wild. I loved them both and enjoyed my time with them but I knew I needed to do more with them since they had so much energy.

Since Katie was still a pup, I didn't go to any JRTCA events with Frankie. I felt that Katie needed to be bigger and then we'd go again. But then the next blow occurred in my life and I got laid off from work. I had two pups and a mortgage but I had savings. I was able to hold things together as I looked for a new job.

My home was a 2 story house with a main floor and upper floor with 3 bedrooms. There was also a partially finished small basement that had a walkout to the back yard. When you walked out, there was a cement slab porch and then wooden stairs that led up to the main floor deck. I put a doggy door on the sliding glass door to the deck off the kitchen so that they could go out and take care of their business.

On this particular day, I was in my bedroom getting ready and I suddenly heard this high pitched squeal and yelp and I ran to the window to look out. Frankie was on the deck and Katie was at the bottom of the stairs holding her leg up and crying. It appeared she had fallen so I raced down 2 flights of stairs to the walkout basement. I flew outside to get her but she had already climbed those wooden stairs to the main floor deck and was sitting at the top looking down at me. She had her right paw raised as she watched me run up and come to her.

I was a bit frantic. "Katie, are you OK?" I asked her, as if she could let me know, but she just sat there looking at me holding her leg up. She didn't make a sound but she let me take her and examine her leg and I knew it was broken. I had to get her to the vet and fast. So I grabbed her up and wrapped her so we could take the trip to the vet. I put Frankie in his kennel and left him at home. I was not sure at that point if he had caused her to fall but my gut told me he may have. She had broken her leg on the tumble down the stairs.

When we got to the vet, we were asked to wait for the doctor in one of the examination rooms. Katie was really quiet and good with me as I held her gently but as soon as the doctor attempted to even touch her, she growled at him, so I had to assist so she would be calm. They took x-rays and came back and told me that she indeed broke her leg and they would need to put a cast on it. They also explained that the break may not heal correctly because of where it broke and she was so young. They put the cast on and sent me off with hopes that it would heal fine and have no issues.

She was the cutest little thing with her cast and it never stopped her from running and having a good time and playing with Frankie. But I catered to my little one and we started to bond even more from this point. The cast came off after six weeks and she was back to her normal self, running, having fun and playing with Frankie.

It appeared she had healed after all.

Three

Still Broken

About six months had passed since Katie got her cast off and I noticed she was starting to limp. The limping was getting progressively worse. I took her everywhere with me, Frankie too. We were at my niece's husband's family's for a get together and my brother asked me why Katie was limping so bad and that's when I realized indeed, she was now limping really bad.

The very next day I called her breeder because I had no money to pay for a vet. I explained what had happened and that she needed to go to the vet and I wondered if she wouldn't help me since I couldn't afford it on my own. She was generous enough to let me use her vet and she paid for the visit. When the vet examined her they explained that this was caused by the break she had gotten when she fell off the deck. Although it had healed now it had caused her right leg to stop growing while her left leg continued to grow. This was causing her bone on her right leg to pull away from her shoulder and was causing her to limp.

I was frantic inside my head! What!?!? How was I going to help my precious dog? They continued and explained that she would need to have surgery. The surgery meant cutting a piece of her bone out of her left leg so that it was the same length as the right leg and then the right leg would be able to go back into her shoulder socket and stop the limping.

I just wanted to cry. How was I going to afford this? I mean, it seemed I was just hitting obstacles on a rather regular basis in my life. I explained my situation and the vet referred me to another vet that would take payments and would be less expensive in the next city south of where I lived. I would have to make it down there for an initial examination and then a second time for the actual surgery. I couldn't not help my dog and although I couldn't afford to do this, I was bound and determined I would figure out a way.

So I scheduled the first appointment and got all the details on what needed to be done. The cost was way over my head but he gave me options that I knew I could juggle and would make it happen for my little sweetheart. I agreed to payment options and scheduled her surgery which meant bringing her back and she would need to spend the night.

I don't remember how I got the money to make the first payment so that they would do the surgery but I can only say that I had wonderful friends that helped and eventually I did pay them all back, including the vet. I also had recently made a new friend online who lived in the city south of me and she let me stay with her while Katie had her surgery.

Katie was back in a cast again but now, she would heal the right way.

Four

Finding Her Job

Katie's leg did heal and she no longer limped. She was running and jumping like she had before and was so happy again. The connection between her and I really began to grow. She was so faithful and I loved her so much! I also had two, not one, Jack Russells and if you know anything about Jacks, they need to have a job! They need a purpose in their life and it can't just be sitting around at home and hanging out in the backyard.

If you do that to them, they are such stubborn, difficult dogs and Frankie fit that to a "T". Katie was always laid back, obedient and always with me. So we started going to the JRTCA events again and this time, I started entering them in trials. I couldn't show Frankie because he had a gray ear but I did show Katie once. She didn't place because her healed leg came with not so perfect confirmation. There were two other events though, that looked like both of my dogs could enjoy.

Racing and Go-to-Ground! Oh yeah! Frankie was in heaven!!! Racing is this long field which has to be at least 150 feet long. Your dog has to be muzzled and placed in a starting box at one end of the course and they race to the other. On the other end, there is a wall of hay bales with a small opening the size of one fat Jack. Out of this hole in the wall is a rope that is as long as the field and is laying there right in front (about five feet away) of the boxed Jacks with a lure (looked like a raccoon tail) tied to it.

Inside these boxes are Jacks barking and crying to get at that lure. Do you see this picture? These dogs go wild chasing this racoon tail down the field and through a hole only ONE dog can fit through at a time. They all converge on that opening at once! It's like the cartoons when you see nothing but dust clouds and exclamation marks. The dogs are barking and going crazy trying to get through the hole (now you know why they were muzzled). Crazy barking dogs! Frankie loved it!!! Katie… not so much. She stopped about three quarters of the way there and looked ahead and then looked back and turned around and came back to me.

Go-to-Ground. What do you think that means? Wooden mazes are set up that the dogs need to get through. They go in one end and can make all the turns they need to but they must come out the other end and bark at a rat in a cage. This maze has escape hatches if the dog can't figure it out. The maze isn't open though, its wooden halls, connected together, encased to simulate a dog going into an actual dirt hole after a badger, for example. Frankie again, was in heaven.

The winner has to get through the maze in a certain amount of time and then bark at the rat for a certain amount of time. Fastest dog that gets through the maze and then barks at the rat long enough wins. Frankie got in there and was at the rat in no time and he barked. He wanted to get that rat so bad! Katie… not so much. She went in and then came out and wondered why I wanted her to do that? But I encouraged her to go but she just wouldn't do it. So I took her to look at the rat to see if that would tempt her to do it, but she wasn't that interested in a caged rat either. She did bark at it but then stopped. It was at one of the trials that I heard about flyball. It wasn't a JRTCA thing but I thought, "Why not check it out?"

Flyball is a relay race for dogs, any breed of dogs. There are two teams of four dogs each that race against each other, the fastest team wins. There are two lanes and in the middle stands the judge. At the end of each lane is a box with a 45 degree angle that when the dog jumps to turn on it, it triggers a tennis ball to fly out that the dog needs to catch and carry all the way back to the other end. In between both ends are huddles that the dogs need to jump. The height of the hurdle is determined by the smallest dog on the team.

Obviously this is not going to be as easy as the JRTCA trials where their natural born instinct just needs to kick in. No, this requires training. So, I signed up Frankie to learn flyball. We all head to the arena where the training is being held and I leave Katie in her kennel and take Frankie out for his lesson.

These initial classes were actually in a small enclosed arena at the fairgrounds so if a dog tried to run free, they didn't go very far. There was an introductory training we had already completed to socialize Frankie and he did pretty well. The first thing to learn was just running to the box and then back to your owner. That's it, just let them go and they run straight ahead to the box and come back. The distance was short at first and then progressively got longer until they could do the whole run and come back to you.

Frankie never got to the box. Frankie never came back to me. Frankie tried to run free. And it was frustrating and really slowed down the class. I spent most of my time chasing Frankie. Three quarters of the way in, I asked if it would be OK to try my other dog and they said "Sure." So I kenneled Frankie and brought in Katie. Katie ran to the box and came back until she could do the entire distance.

The following week, we were back and Frankie was getting trained again. But half way through the class after chasing him down every time I let him go, everyone was getting frustrated including me. I again asked about letting Katie try and they said OK again. In this class, they were now jumping the hurdles and going to the box and coming back. This time, they also learned to hit the box, catch the ball and come back holding the ball all the way. By the end of that class, Katie could do the whole thing. She excelled at this job and she loved it! She was already ahead of most of the dogs in the class.

It's the third week of training and I show up with Frankie. Immediately, Frankie's trying to run free again. He would not listen at all. I asked the instructor if I could let Katie train instead? This time she told me that I had to choose between the dogs because only one could continue to be trained. So I put Frankie back in his kennel and Katie started learning how to be really good at flyball. Katie loved it!!

Now imagine that teams are looking for the fastest small dog they can find.

Five

Learning to Fly

Katie had a job and although I tried several times with Frankie, this just wasn't what he wanted to do. We went through all the training which was always working on hitting the box at a turn and grabbing the ball in the air as they were turning and racing back to the starting line so that the next dog could go. The next dog had to wait for the returning dog to cross that start line before it could cross that same start line on their way to the box. This requires timing the release of your dog so they are at full run when they cross the start line and not before the other dog does on their way back from the box.

Once Katie got through the first training session, she moved on to perfecting her turn and working on timing her release. I would chase her all the way to the start line so she was at full speed when she crossed. She seemed to float over the hurdles and if she missed catching the ball, she always retrieved it before she would return to me. Other dogs would just come back and that didn't count when you raced. She never dropped the ball on the way back either because that didn't count either.

I would scream at her as I was chasing her to the start line and scream at her as she ran to the box encouraging her to go fast and get that ball. And then I would scream at her to come back and come back fast.

Since she would be flying at her fastest coming back as well, I had a three foot long tug toy that I waited at the start line with and started running away from her as she jumped the last hurdle. She would race harder when I did this to cross the start (now finish) line and drop the ball and race to get the tug. Once she had it, she clamped on and I would swing her around, off the ground and stop her momentum and we'd tug for a bit and then we were done with that particular heat. The ball acted as the primary motivator to run to the box and the tug was the secondary motivator to pass that finish line.

We progressed to doing demonstration shows for the flyball club in order to attract more members and then the best thing happened, we were asked to join one of the flyball teams. This meant going to flyball competitions not only locally but in other parts of our state and out of state. It was a really good time for me and my Katie-mate. I used to always call her my Katie-mate. Katie was always with me. We were always doing things together. We even flew to a tournament and she was always so good. In fact, they didn't even notice I had carried a dog onto the plane since she was quiet as a mouse.

I had to get gear for her and, by this time, I had gotten another job. I had held onto my home but my savings had been drained so the job was my only source of money. Luckily, it was only myself and my dogs and what I earned was more than sufficient to take care of us and start to rebuild my savings.

I purchased her a nice larger kennel that broke down so I could carry it with me to the tournaments. She had a small fan to keep her cool and I would cover her kennel when she wasn't racing so she could rest. Flyball tournaments are quite noisy with all the barking dogs. Katie was always quiet as a mouse until she knew she would be racing and then she would start barking her head off on the way to the track.

When we did our flyball tournaments, I would massage Katie between heats and take her to the pool after runs to cool off. We were bonded completely by now. The dogs were not allowed to soil during a race so between heats, I would always take her to do her business and she learned to do it when I asked her to. On our way home, she would sit on my lap and tuck her head under my chin and just ride there close to my heart. We would go hiking and I could have her off leash and it was wonderful. She always listened and was always with me. I had started dating again but nothing serious so my dogs were my world, especially Katie.

Our first team was a great starter team but we were not the fastest and then a tragedy occurred. The border collie on our team was struck by a car and passed. That was when our team folded and we were all very upset about the loss. Eventually though, we all got on other teams and Katie and I actually got on a really good team where she was the only small dog. During that time, she was making the course in just under five seconds, her very best racing times.

I also decided to get more involved in flyball and became a judge for the racing. I loved it and Katie was in heaven.

Katie seriously appeared to fly as she raced the course.

Six

Adding the Family

I had only been working for my new job for six months when I got laid off again. This was a more devastating blow since I no longer had any savings to speak of and there had not been enough time to build it either. This was the third layoff I had while working in the industry I was in, so I thought to myself, I needed to do something different. I started working from home selling educational material to make ends meet. I had one good month where I made $5000 but that never happened again since I am definitely no sales woman. I had eventually drained the little savings I had rebuilt and had to stop making payments on my house but I never stopped trying to keep it together.

During this time I also started dating again, online dating. I met so many people but none grew into anything more than an acquaintance. I was really struggling financially too. I no longer could afford to put gas in my car or buy groceries. Friends and family helped me when they could, especially my parents. Then I met the person I would build a new family with and she had dogs of her own.

Katie and I still were doing flyball but it seemed to always be a conflict with the new person in my life. Demonstrations got harder for me to get to and eventually, I quit the flyball club. We did get into another club but I had begun to notice that Katie's determination to be the best would sometimes cause her to overheat so I needed her to slow down. I needed to make sure she stayed healthy. And then I started to notice that her leg was starting to hurt her from hitting that box at such high speeds so another reason we needed to back off a bit. We only stayed with the club for one season and then we stopped flyball altogether.

Maybe it was really just the fact that my new partner took more of my time than Katie did. Katie was still always with me but we stopped doing flyball and hiking and she became a stay at home dog. She never complained. Eventually I sold my home and moved in with my new partner. On a trip to Yellowstone, we had my partner's friend watch our dogs and on the last day of the trip before we had headed home, we found out that Frankie had gotten out of the yard and was hit by a car. That hurt my heart and it was a bit somber going home!

Even though I only had Katie now, I also now had a partner and two other dogs. I got a new job, working for the same folks I do today. I was always busy running around or taking care of the house or working late. Katie was with me when I was at home but we were no longer doing things together as we had before. The one thing we always did was, I would pitch the ball for her so she could retrieve it. I set up a small pool off to the side so when she got hot she would dive into the pool and sit a bit before she brought the ball back. She could go on like this for hours but I normally only did it for about an hour so her leg wouldn't be too sore. This became what we did together besides always being near each other.

She was such a good dog. When I needed her to do her business I would put her outside and tell her to "be clean." She would run around and then look up at me but she hadn't gone so I would tell her again, "Be clean, Katie." So she would run around some more and then look up at me again but still she had not done her business. So I would be more firm, "Katie. Be clean." She would then run around, squat and do her numbers. I praised her and had her come back in so she could be with me. We did this often, it seemed like a game she played with me just to make sure I was paying attention to her.

My partner and I eventually bought a house together and then we decided to have children. We adopted our son via social services and now I was really busy with the family and working. During this time, my partner's German Shepherd passed, Katie became the alpha of the house. But my partner went out the very next day and bought another puppy of the same breed. We still had three dogs, my little Katie-mate, her other German Shepherd that was about the same age as Katie and the new puppy, Gypsy.

Katie was also getting older.

Seven

The Blind Eye

Our son had chronic lung disease so he was on oxygen seven by twenty-four and had a feeding tube that had to be changed every two weeks. Whenever we went anywhere, we had to make sure to take his tanks and food. He slept with a pulse-ox which would go off almost every hour on the hour. It was our dream to have children and we had tried to do it naturally so many times but it never happened so, we decided to adopt.

Katie was still with me and always by my side but now I didn't have the time I used to spend with her. We adopted our son a year after we started fostering him. Six months after that, we started fostering two more boys since we wanted him to have siblings. A year and half later we adopted those two boys and their baby sister and our family grew to four kids, three dogs, a cat and two adults.

Katie was graying by now but what I hadn't noticed or maybe, I turned a blind eye to it since, I was so busy. She wasn't only getting really gray, she was getting really thin. My partner mentioned it to me at one time but I just thought it was her old age and all would be fine but then Katie started puking more after she would eat but she never complained or cried so things kept going as normal.

I'm not sure if it's good or bad to fill your life with too much but in retrospect, I think it's not really the best thing to do. I mean, you start to miss the quality of things in your life that used to bring you such joy. You know, like spending quality time with my Katie-mate. I no longer had her with me all the time, I left her at home a lot. I traveled with my job so I wasn't always there. My partner would tell me that she would always lay on my things and wouldn't let anyone come near them. She would stay by the front door until I returned no matter where I went, whether it was to go to work for the day or take a business trip for two weeks. She was always my faithful little Katie-mate.

I remember thinking when I would have issues with my partner how it would be so nice if Katie was the human in my life but she was my dog. The best dog I had ever had and I loved her so much but I let my life take control of me instead of being in control of it.

After my partner told me a second time that she thought Katie looked too thin, I looked at her and didn't really realize just how thin she really had become. I made a mental note to take her to the vet but I never did, I was just too busy. Soon, Katie started puking more and more but still never did she complain. She still stayed by my side when I was home and protected my belongings when I wasn't.

Right before Christmas, our older German Shepherd, Buffy got so bad with her hips that she could no longer stand up. We made the hard decision to put her down. We had our vet come to the house to check on her and he said it was time to put her down as well. All of our kids were there and we all said our good-byes and then he gave her that shot and she passed peacefully in her sleep.

The vet took her body and as a family we cried and mourned for our Buffy dog. She was a gentle spirit and never haggled with anyone.

I held my children that night and Katie stayed by my side.

Eight

Saying Goodbye

olding Katie that night, I realized she really had gotten thin, really thin. She was small and frail. I started noticing that she was puking every day now and had lost way too much weight. I was still so busy but my intention now was to get her to the vet, no matter what. It was only one week after Buffy had passed when I woke and Katie was too weak to get out of her kennel.

My heart sank and we were headed to the vet but first she let me bathe her and clean her up. She did not smell good at all. Thinking back, I probably shouldn't have done that but she let me all the same. She always trusted me so completely.

I called my sister and she came with me. I knew as frail as she had become that they wouldn't be able to help her but I tried to be positive and hope for the best. Just maybe they could save her.

When we got there, the vet examined her and made a comment on how frail she was but she said we could try to help her but it would only prolong the inevitable. We should really consider putting her down. Even as I type these words, I am crying because I loved that dog so very much. She was my Katie-mate and I had let her down. I had stopped noticing that she had needed me and I wasn't there for her. She trusted me all her life and I had not noticed she had gotten sick. It turned out that her kidneys had started to fail her and it was really way too late to bring her back.

I sat with Katie on my lap and I needed to make a decision. She looked up at me and I knew, I knew she was telling me to let her go. She was in pain and she was ready to go and now I needed to let her. She never stopped looking at me. I held her close, I cried, I told her I knew she wanted to go and I would let her. I kept her with me for what seemed like an hour before I got the courage to tell the vet that it was OK to put her down. My sister sat there with me, she was also crying.

When the vet came back, I let her know that we would put her down. She gave Katie a shot to relax her as I held her for the last time. I couldn't stop crying, I couldn't stop feeling guilty that I had let this happen to her. I had let her down.

Finally, I handed Katie to the vet and she took her away to give her that final shot. We sat in the examination room for another half hour before I could bring myself to leave and I was so glad my sister had been there for me.

I said goodbye to my Katie-mate, with tears streaming down my cheeks, barely being able to breath in hopes I could pull myself together. For weeks after, I cried for her, for my loss and for my guilt, for my negligence but I know Katie never held it against me, she had loved me unconditionally. She was the best dog I could have ever hoped to have.

My precious Katie-mate was in heaven.

Nine

Always in my Heart

Katie was born on March 29, 2003 and passed away on December 14, 2016. She was 13 years old or 91 human years. I posted her passing on social media with the following:

In loving memory of Kaitlyn "Katie" Elizabeth. The best friend and companion anyone could have been blessed with. You will be missed my sweet little girl and will always hold a special place in my heart.

Katie touched my heart so deeply that even after over five years since she passed, I mourn for her. Thinking of her still brings tears to my eyes and I cry. I still miss her so much because she was such a wonderful dog, such a wonderful companion who was always there for me even when I wasn't for her. I still feel guilty that I didn't notice she was in pain at the end of her time here and I didn't do something sooner. And although the vet had told me that dogs rarely ever recover from kidney failure I still feel guilty that I had not done more for my Katie-mate. But I will always have the most wonderful memories of a dog that stole my heart and was just plain awesome.

Katie had deep dark black eyes that reached into my very soul and spoke to me. We had a special connection and love and she honored that until the end and this is my way of honoring her. To share her story with you so you too can know she existed and was the best friend and companion a person could ever hope for from the canine community.

May you rest in peace Katie-mate. I imagine you young again, racing to get that tennis ball. Running back and then taking a detour to jump into a pool of cool water where you sit and pant. Then you jump out again to bring me the ball so you can do it over and over and over again. Be free my sweet little love and be waiting for me when I join you in the future, that way I know where I am when I get there.

Love you Katie!